First Field Trips

Aquarium

by Cari Meister

Bullfrog
Books

Ideas for Parents and Teachers

Bullfrog Books let children practice reading informational text at the earliest reading levels. Repetition, familiar words, and photo labels support early readers.

Before Reading

- Discuss the cover photo. What does it tell them?
- Look at the picture glossary together. Read and discuss the words.

Read the Book

- "Walk" through the book and look at the photos. Let the child ask questions. Point out the photo labels.
- Read the book to the child, or have him or her read independently.

After Reading

- Prompt the child to think more. Ask: Have you ever been to an aquarium? What was your favorite animal?

Bullfrog Books are published by Jump!
5357 Penn Avenue South
Minneapolis, MN 55419
www.jumplibrary.com

Library of Congress Cataloging-in-Publication Data

Meister, Cari, author.
 Aquarium / by Cari Meister.
    pages cm. — (First field trips)
 Audience: Ages 5–8.
 Audience: K to grade 3.
 Summary: "Vibrant photographs and carefully leveled text take emergent readers on a trip to an aquarium, introducing them to a variety of lake and ocean life. Includes picture glossary and index."
—Provided by publisher.
 Includes bibliographical references and index.
 ISBN 978-1-62031-292-6 (hardcover: alk. paper) —
 ISBN 978-1-62496-358-2 (ebook)
1. Public aquariums—Juvenile literature.
2. Aquarium animals—Juvenile literature.
3. School field trips—Juvenile literature. I. Title.
 QL78.M37 2016
 597.073—dc23
                                        2015030637

Editor: Jenny Fretland VanVoorst
Series Designer: Ellen Huber
Book Designer: Lindaanne Donohoe
Photo Researcher: Lindaanne Donohoe

Photo Credits: All photos by Shutterstock except: Alamy, 16–17; Corbis, 10; f11photo/Shutterstock, 5, 8–9; iStock, 11, 14, 15, 20–21.

Printed in the United States of America at Corporate Graphics in North Mankato, Minnesota.

Table of Contents

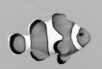

Tank Time!

Where is the class going?

To the aquarium!

Wow!

The saltwater tank is big.

It has ocean animals.

Di sees a whale shark.

It is the biggest shark.

It eats tiny things.

It eats fish eggs.

9

Here is a sea turtle.
It is five feet
(1.5 meters) long.

It has flippers.
They help it swim.

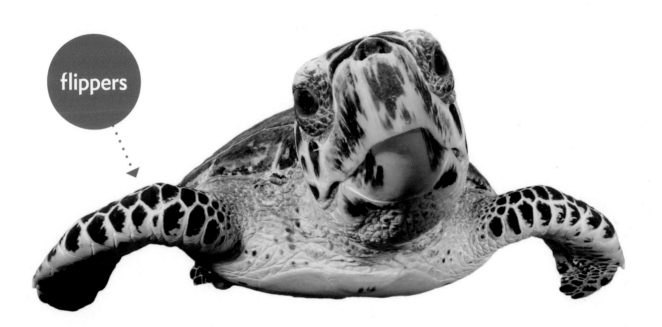

flippers

This animal has flippers, too.

It is a scuba diver!

He cleans the tank.

He feeds the animals.

In the wild, animals hunt.

Workers feed animals here.
That way they do not eat
each other.

Joe sees a
freshwater tank.

It has lake fish.

Ty pets a stingray.

He is kind.

He uses a flat hand.

What a fun day!

Animals at the Aquarium

shark

anemone

fish

coral

Picture Glossary

flipper
A broad, flat limb or shoe used for swimming.

saltwater
Water that is salty, like the ocean.

freshwater
Water that is not salty, like inland lakes.

scuba diver
A person who swims underwater using special breathing gear.

Index

To Learn More

Learning more is as easy as 1, 2, 3.

1) Go to www.factsurfer.com

2) Enter "aquarium" into the search box.

3) Click the "Surf" button to see a list of websites.

With factsurfer.com, finding more information is just a click away.